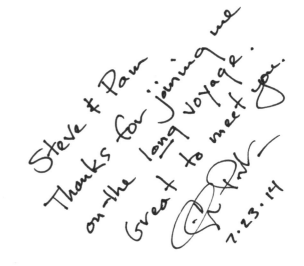

Steve & Paw
Thanks for joining me
on the long voyage.
Great to meet you.

7.23.14

MISTY FJORDS

NATIONAL MONUMENT WILDERNESS

CHIP PORTER

JACK AND BRUCE JOHNSTONE were raised in the rugged back country of East Behm Canal, an area now known as Misty Fjords. Life wasn't easy in the wilderness in the 1920's and 30's, but as both men told me, times were good, and there was always an exciting adventure waiting just around the corner. They prospected, fished, and hand-logged in the summer and guided big-game hunters and trapped fur in the colder months. Living along the Canal was about having a roaring fire in the wood stove, a mulligan stew in the pot, and card games after dinner. Their father "Daddy" Johnstone told them, "you measure your wealth not by money but by how many friends you have." ✐ The brothers were unequalled woodsmen with amazing skills and a lifetime of practical knowledge. In the early 1930's they pulled and poled two heavily loaded river boats 45 miles up the Unuk River to Sulphurets Creek, an almost unbelievable feat. With a summer's worth of supplies, they prospected their way inland, following a trail of fine gold dust. Their dream of finding the "mother lode" ended in a melt pond below the towering face of a nameless calving glacier. Years later, after the ice had receded, Canadian geologists discovered huge gold deposits there. The lake the glacier left behind was named Brucejack Lake in their honor. ✐ Both men were decades older than I, yet from the day we met I felt trusted, looked upon as an equal, and treated like an old friend.

2

Brucejack Lake.

ACKNOWLEDGMENTS

I have many people to thank. ✎ First and foremost are three guys who have pushed me for years to do a book on Misty Fjords: the infamously fishy/dinosaur artist Ray Troll; bush pirate—I mean bush pilot—Dave Doyon; and photographer extraordinaire Mark Kelley. These pals of mine never stopped with their mantra, do a book, do a book, do a book. Thanks, Ray, for your faith in my ability, Dave, ol' buddy, for everything, and Mark for being so generous with your knowledge. ✎ Thanks in no particular order to the many wonderful people who've helped me. Some gave the gift of flight while others gave the gift of opportunity. Here, too, are a few souls whose deep appreciation for my work gave me the faith I needed to make this book. ✎ Terry and Cheri Pyles, Evon Zerbetz, Chris Urstaad, Sue Medel, Dan and Mary Ann Fiehrer, George Shaffer, Bill Fowler, Wayne Williams, Gus-Gus Peterson, Michelle Troll, Chuck Slagle, Bobbi Anderson, Deb Clark, Lesley Kamm, Bob Widness, Amy Holm, Marty Loken, Candy Peterson, Mary Ida Henrikson, Hall Anderson, my always supportive mom and dad, Carl and Marly Porter, and my daughter Andrea Wargi, who would rather have a picture for Christmas than money! ✎ Special thanks to Misty Fjords Air, Taquan Air, RdM Air Service, Carlin Air, SeaWind Aviation, Pro-Mech Air and Island Wings. Double special thanks to gifted wordsmith Nick Jans. Without Nick, this book might have slewed dangerously off in any direction. I guess the final straw was the day he and Mark Kelley barged into my house, told me to sit down, shut up, and listen. They yelled, "you're going to do a book on Misty Fjords!" "And I'm going to write it !" Nick threatened. ✎ Nick actually had the unenviable job of being my editor. Be sure you thank him when you see him. ✎ Ten months later the book went to press. ✎ Thanks to all (and especially all those I forgot).

—Chip Porter

Ketchikan, Alaska, gateway to Misty Fjords National Monument Wilderness.

Fjord; (*also fiord*): ❧ A long, narrow, deep inlet of the sea between high cliffs, as in Norway and Iceland, typically formed by submergence of a glaciated valley. ❧ This dictionary definition is greatly simplified; it would take many pages to explain the complete evolution of Misty Fjords. In a nutshell, the colliding North American plate and the counter-rotating Pacific plate caused broken crustal fragments to fuse together and lift up to form the Coastal Mountain Batholith, now known as the Coast Range. Intense pressure between the two plates melted solid rock, causing volcanic activity to surface throughout the Monument. Eons of wind and rain eroded deep, V-shaped valleys in the up-lifted mass, leaving serrated ridgelines and jagged peaks. ❧ As weather shifts grew colder, years of accumulated alpine snow compressed into solid ice. The weight became so immense the ice began to flow downhill. Millions of years and dozens of mild to freezing climate cycles later, glaciers had gouged, scraped, and plowed the mountains away, leaving the rounded tops, wider U-shaped valleys, and deep canyon fjords seen in the Mistys today. ❧ The most severe ice age on record, the Pleistocene, peaked a mere twenty thousand years ago. The Monument was completely buried under an ice plateau 4000 feet deep on the western edge, and over 6000 feet high in the east. Only a handful of spiky mountain tops called Nunatuks were left untouched. Scientists tell us this vast ice field stretched all the way across the continent to Cape Cod on the Atlantic Ocean.

Walker Cove.

Punchbowl Wall between rain squalls, Rudyerd Bay

Big country—for perspective, find the yellow tent in the lower left.

Sunlight and shadows, Rudyerd Bay.

Abstract designs in fractured granite.

First Canyon, Unuk River.

Rudyerd Bay.

There are basically only two ways to get around in Misty Fjords. One is by boat, which gives a definite, head-thrown-back, oh-my-gosh perspective of the towering granite cliffs and steep, snow-covered peaks. Throw in lots of fresh air and plenty of room to move about, and you'll understand why cruising is a great way to go. High-speed catamarans carry you safely up Behm Canal and into massive, glacier-carved Rudyerd Bay.

Two is to fly. There is nothing quite like flying the Mistys in a de Havilland Beaver. These tough, boxy seaplanes thunder in and out of remote and otherwise unreachable mountain passes with the reliability of an old friend, as mile after mile of sparkling lakes, cascading waterfalls and fractured, treeless ridges pass beneath your wide-eyed view. Which way should you travel? It comes down to personal choice. Both trips are exceptional adventures, and you can't go wrong.

SeaWind Aviation's Beaver floatplane flies past towering cliffs.

A glacial erratic near the edge of the 2200-foot Amphitheater Wall, Rudyerd Bay. 16

Sealevel Creek flows across the western border of the Monument, Revillagigedo Island.

Hand-split cedar shake trail.

Avalanche path in fall colors.

Evening light blankets an island covered with muskeg ponds and bull pine trees, Punchbowl Lake.

Flight-seeing floatplanes, One-Eyed Creek, Rudyerd Bay.

Harding Point, at the northern tip of Smeaton Island, Short Pass, East Behm Canal.

Johnny Kristovich at Tombstone Bay.

Misty Fjords was far more populated in the past than it is now. Two hundred years ago Tlingit Indian villages thrived at Tongass Island, Kirk Point, and Kah Shakes Cove. Summer fish camps bustled with activity at Checates Cove, Mink Bay, and Point Whaley. Ingenious stone fish traps bordered nearly every major fish stream. In 1862 the horrors of smallpox decimated thousands of these aboriginal people, and the survivors were forced to leave their tainted homesites.

By the late nineteen hundreds, opportunistic white men came north to mine gold and log the majestic stands of towering old-growth red cedar and Sitka spruce. The building of a small salmon cannery on the Klahini River was soon followed by prosperous, state-of-the-art facilities at Roe Point, Hidden Inlet, and Boca de Quadra. During the tough years of the Great Depression, homesteaders moved into the Fjords, hoping to supplement their meager incomes by hand-logging, trapping, and even farming. In East Behm Canal the Kickerbockers, Johnstones, Morgans and Bald-Headed Mike Perez all built sturdy cabins. The Wolfs lived at the mouth of the Chickamin River and the Matney Ranch was located on the Unuk River's fertile tidal plain. The Starrish Clan had a summer camp at the mouth of Rudyerd Bay, while the Kristovich family lived year round at Tombstone, on the Portland Canal.

23   The half-circle of rocks at center is an ancient Indian fish trap. Others, eroded by time, lead off to the upper right.

Mink Bay, Boca de Quadra.

Fast forward to the twenty-first century. In this constantly damp country, nothing lasts. The log homes have melted back into the earth, leaving only shards of broken glass and rusty nails behind. The canneries, once the best technology money could buy, are now beaches skewered with blackened piling stubs and littered with fading bricks and rusted hunks of decaying metal. No one lives year round in the Misty Fjords anymore. Pick a late fall or winter day and you'll probably have the entire Monument all to yourself. Walk any beach and the only tracks you'll run across belong to birds or animals. It wasn't always this way. Know with certainty some hardy soul in hob-nailed boots has walked the path ahead of you, a hundred years or more ago.

Campfire coals.

Hanging glacier, McQuillan Ridge.

A lake with no name in the middle of nowhere . . .

and cliffs that go down so far it looks like up

North end of the Punchbowl/Amphitheater ridge, Rudyerd Bay.

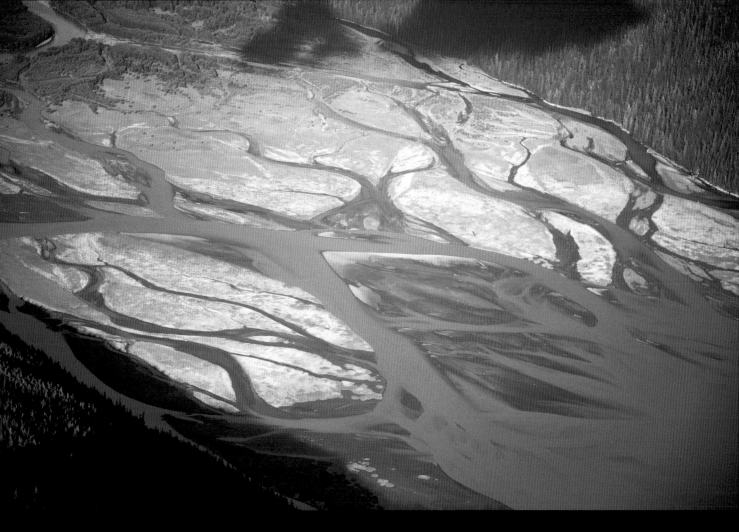

The silt-filled Unuk River flats, Burroughs Bay

The verdant underbelly of a prickly devils club thicket.

Spruce trees, drowned when a landslide blocked Mirror Lake's outlet.

Two days after 9/11/2001, my friend Keith Smith and I climbed an unnamed peak that sits high above Punchbowl Lake. We spent the night peering out over the silent, starlit landscape. Occasionally we talked, but mostly we just sat and looked, quiet in our sorrow. As dawn progressed, our spirits were lifted by a dazzling and most welcome sunrise. ✍ The spectacular, mostly vertical "Punchbowl" is normally abuzz in September. Vintage floatplanes roar overhead and high-powered cruise boats carve the waters below. Nothing moved that day, nothing—no boats, no planes, not even a high-flying jet. If it wasn't for our space-age camping gear it could have been 1901 instead.

Sunrise, Punchbowl Lake.

Sundog, Foggy Bay, Revillagigedo Channel.

Misty Fjords Air's Cessna 185, above the Coast Range at sundown.

Mountain hemlock trees in alpine snow, Revillagigedo Island.

Fall colors on beaver ponds, mile twelve, Chickamin River.

It's a vertical place. Walker Cove.

Granite ridges, Rudyerd Bay.

Unnamed canyon, Peabody Mountains.

Many wonderfully adapted birds and animals inhabit the Monument. Agile mountain goats dot unclimbable cliffs and hoary marmots whistle warnings in high, treeless valleys. Land otter are sleek swimmers whose table fare is fresh seafood of any kind, while beaver are content to gnaw bark from willow and alder branches. Wolverine are bone-crunching carnivores that hunt and scavenge. Their much smaller cousin, the once-coveted mink, is a fierce predator that eats virtually anything it can kill. Bald eagles, great horned owls, ptarmigans, red-tailed hawks, grouse, ravens, crows, kingfishers, woodpeckers, and many types of waterfowl add year-round avian beauty. Canadian geese, trumpeter swans, hummingbirds, chickadees, jays, juncos, robins, swallows, mallards, teal, and scores of other birds and ducks come and go as their migration patterns cross the 56th parallel. Two species of bear thrive in the Mistys, the great Alaskan brown bear and the smaller black. Both favor salmon streams, grassy tidal flats, and berry-covered hillsides. Either bear will dine on tiny crabs, plant roots, skunk cabbage, grass, seals, dead whales, dying salmon, or anything else they can sniff or dig up. Any stream in the Fjords big enough to attract fish or a few dungeness crab will have a harbor seal or two swimming back and forth at its mouth. New Eddystone

Granite cliffs meet rain forest, Rudyerd Bay.

Rock and the Channel Islands are great places to view seals high and dry. Here they congregate in large, semi-camouflaged groups to rest and sleep on special rocks and beaches known as haul-outs. Being surrounded by water protects them from hungry bear and wolves, but occasionally marauding transient killer whale packs reduce their numbers. Alaskan gray wolves and Sitka black-tailed deer both live and die in the Monument. One evening I anchored a yacht touring Misty Fjords in a small, protected bight near the mainland and shut down the engines. Early the next morning we were having our first cup of coffee when someone heard the sound of howling wolves, which got closer and closer. Suddenly a deer burst from the woods, ran down the beach into the water, and began to swim determinedly toward an island in the distance. As it passed the back of the quiet motor yacht, the automatic generator kicked on with the tat-tat-tat-tat of water-cooled exhaust. The confused deer corkscrewed around and headed back the way it had come. We watched open-mouthed as it stumbled up the beach and disappeared into the woods. Moments later the whole cove rang with howls. After a short time, a lone wolf came trotting across the beach, a bloody foreleg dangling from its jaws. Walk a few steps into this forest, and you realize without a doubt true wilderness is alive and well.

Porcupine in a spruce tree, Eulachon River.

The deepest corner of this overhang is always dry and windless, a fine place to build a fire in a rainstorm.

47   **Fresh powder avalanches in Walker Cove.**   **The essence of Misty Fjords.**

RdM Air Service, July, Manzoni Lake.

The Monument's western boundary goes through upper Fish Creek, Revillagigedo Island.

In the past, sturdy stumps called "tail-holts" were used to help drag logs through the old-growth forest.

The week after Christmas is a great time to have Misty Fjords all to yourself. This particular year the weather was gray, rainy, slushy, and for the most part miserable. On the fifth day I was putting around in my skiff near the head of the Walker Cove, thinking seriously about giving up my photo quest and heading back to Ketchikan in time for New Year's Eve. About an hour before nightfall the weather finally began to clear and I took the picture on the opposite page. ✐ Was the one image worth all the time and effort? You bet.

Waterfalls literally drop out of the clouds, Walker Cove.

Walker Cove, December 30th.

In winter, drifting snows blanket this area so heavily there is absolutely no trace of a lake.

New Eddystone Rock surrounded by early morning fog, Behm Canal.

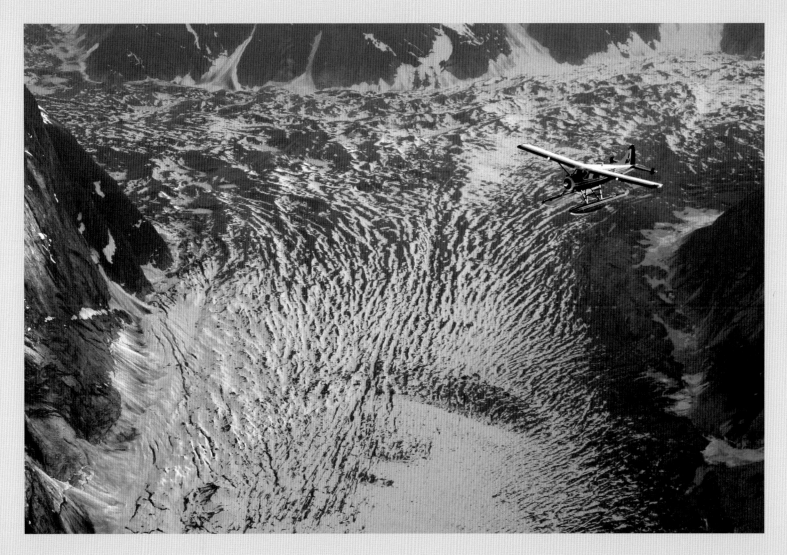

Most glaciers in the Coast Range are melting away.

Eddystone Rock on the lowest tide of the year, taken from 4000 feet.

New Eddystone under a full moon.

But how many pictures can you take of Eddystone?" one of my photographer buddies asked, shaking his head. "As many as I can, a lifetime's worth," I replied. Formally known as New Eddystone Rock, this remarkable, gravity-defying 230 foot pillar of crumbling basalt and rain forest greenery looks different every time I see it. Sitting smack dab in the middle of a four-mile-wide fjord and surrounded by over six hundred feet of water, Eddystone Rock seems completely out of place. A rip in the earth's crust allowed magma to push up and out through cracks in the floor of Behm Canal. Long after the miles of molten lava had solidified, great glaciers advanced and retreated, bulldozing away all but the central core. This volcanic plug, an extraordinary remnant of the Pliocene era, was left behind. ✍ Eddystone seems a spiritual place, and looking back in time, one can certainly imagine it being held in awe by indigenous people. Years ago, laying on my back late one night on the pumice gravel spit, I was treated to the vision of a towering dark monolith surrounded by glowing stars, a heady experience that's vivid, even today. ✍ P.S. Back in my commercial fishing days I almost ran my salmon troller right smack into Eddystone Rock one flat calm sunny day, but that's another story.

Indian paintbrush.

Arctic lupine.

Bunchberry dogwood.

Island Wings, Punchbowl Wall, Rudyerd Bay.

Fog pours out of Punchbowl Cove, Rudyerd Bay.

Wayne Williams enjoys a campfire at the "Shroon Hole," Manzanita Bay.

Light from a roaring fire and a cresting moon.

Midday snow squall, Rudyerd Island, East Behm Canal.

There's a peak in Rudyerd Bay I call Bruce Mountain. My friend Bruce Johnstone told me about a ridge where a fellow might actually manage to climb from salt water all the way to the heady alpine and rocky summit beyond. Bruce, who passed away at 97, grew up as a boy in the Fjords. He told me, "it's probably the easiest place in Rudyerd to get to the top. You won't have any problem." ✐ Here's what my diary says about the climb which I've made twice. "Standing alone on top of this tangled mess of slippery rock and brambles, I feel big apprehension about getting down safely and yet I'm totally elated about being here." and "What a nasty piece of work, a round trip with nothing broken is a major success!" ✐ Bruce would say, "they just don't make 'em like they used to."

Evening from the summit of Bruce Mountain.

A worth-the-climb sunrise from Bruce Mountain.

Sunlit trees reflect light onto the waters of Handlogger Creek, Revillagigedo Island.

The Punchbowl/Amphitheater ridge from the south, Rudyerd Bay.

Part of the Amphitheater Wall with Point Louise in the distance, Rudyerd Bay

A large male "billy" mountain goat in a field of bell heather, Revillagigedo Island.

Between us, bush pilot Dave Doyon and I have spent 65 years kicking around Misty Fjords. We've flown it, boated it, and climbed on it, but at nearly 2.3 million acres (that's 3570 square miles, or over two Rhode Islands), we still haven't seen it all. ✍ Last fall we journeyed to the remote northwest corner of the Monument, looking for volcanoes. We'd seen the Blue River lava flow and teal-green Blue Lake, but neither of us had flown the valley above 2000 feet. This trip, Dave made the turn up Lava Fork at 6000 feet, and the 5433-foot Lava Fork volcano came into view. Roughly 150 years ago, volcanic ash and tephra splattered across icy, snow-covered ridges and spilled down the steep-sided mountains. Accumulating lava slowly pushed its way down a glacier-carved corridor and across the steaming valley floor, thousands of feet below. ✍ Once again, Dave and I just shook our heads in amazement. We continue to be blown away by this savagely beautiful country, every time we visit.

Part of the Lava Fork flow.

Pyroclastic debris on the ridges around Lava Fork volcano.

Carlin Air's de Havilland Beaver over Punchbowl Lake.

Ella Creek.

Alpine valley, Adams Mountains.

Dawn on the summit of the Punchbowl/Amphitheater ridge, Rudyerd Bay.

Watching a winter sunrise light up the ice fog, Handlogger Cove, East Behm Canal.

Misty Fjords Monument is crisscrossed with hundreds of swift-running streams and several high-volume rivers. Five species of salmon—king, pink, coho, sockeye, and chum—follow unseen trails back to the pure, unspoiled waters of their birth. It's not an easy journey, especially the last few miles. Sport and commercial fishermen work certain points and passes. Seals, sea-lions, and killer whales methodically eat their way through the returning schools as well. Year after year the gauntlet's run, and despite the odds, millions of salmon make it back to spawn again. Bottom fish too, are plentiful and lingcod, halibut, yellow-eye rockfish, and rockcod are common saltwater catches. Freshwater lakes hold arctic grayling, eastern brook, rainbow, and cutthroat trout. Prized steelhead and aggressive dolly varden char thrive in either fresh or salt water. Misty Fjords is truly a fisherman's paradise.

King, pink, coho, and chum salmon all spawn in the Wilson River.

Spawned out male pink salmon . . .

and a spawned out male chum salmon.

Purse seiner Rio Grande fishes Revillagigedo Channel.

Harris Point and the mainland mountains behind Smeaton Bay, East Behm Canal.

Sunset over Dixon Entrance.

A killer whale, with bull kelp hanging over its tail, guards her calf.

I missed the pictograph completely my first two or three trips to Burroughs Bay. In my defense, the silty gray-green waters of the fast-moving Unuk River were still flowing down the east side of the valley in those days. ◢ One warm spring morning in 1973, Bruce Johnstone and I left our camp on the Unuk and boated down through the low water maze of greening sandbars and steaming mud flats. We were headed out to Grant Creek, hoping to set some crab pots and look for fresh beaver sign. Near the outside edge of the river's delta, Bruce motioned me to slow down. He then pointed to a small, ivory-colored cliff where an artistic rendition of the sun had been carefully painted. "I was here in 1924, nearly 50 years ago. It looks just as bright today as it did then," he said. ◢ Old timers back in the 1920's told Bruce they thought the ancient painting was a road sign meaning "path to the sun." Indeed, this particular river valley goes from the wet maritime rain forests, through the formidable mountains of the Coast Range, and into the sunny, semi-arid, desert country of the Interior beyond.

Cow parsnips cover the Unuk River mud flats.

Cloud patterns on upper East Behm Canal.

Trees and fog.

RdM Air Service's Beaver passes Walker Cove.

A Dall's porpoise surfs the bow wave of a fishing boat, East Behm Canal.

Star trails and a pre-dawn glow blend over an alpine pond in this four-hour time exposure.

Reflections, Punchbowl Lake

There are times when I spend four or five days out, alone. Surrounded by solitude, I can focus on the world around me in a way that isn't possible otherwise. Here, in front of the old abandoned Tree Point lighthouse, I was miles from any human settlement. I could feel the cool dampness of the dense early morning fog and smell the iodine bite of kelp at low tide. Slate-colored surf made muted, crashing sounds, and ravens kaw-kawed in the distance. ✒ Photography is definitely a loner sport, but it sharpens your senses and it's great stuff for the soul.

An Alaska sword fern, Winstanley Island.

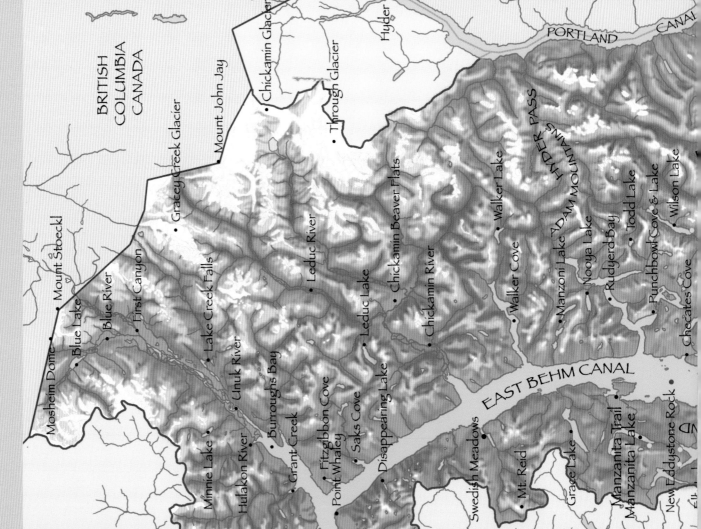

MISTY FJORDS

NATIONAL MONUMENT WILDERNESS

BRITISH
COLUMBIA
CANADA

Chickamin Glacier

Hyder

PORTLAND CANAL

Through Glacier

Mount John Jay

Gracey Creek Glacier

HYDER PASS

ADAM MOUNTAINS

Walker Lake

Leduc River

Chickamin Beaver Flats

Manzoni Lake

Nooya Lake

Rudyerd Bay

Todd Lake

Punchbowl Cove & Lake

Wilson Lake

Mount Stoeckl

First Canyon

Blue River

Blue Lake

Lake Creek Falls

Leduc Lake

Chickamin River

Walker Cove

Checates Cove

Mosheim Dome

Unuk River

Chickamin River

EAST BEHM CANAL

Minnie Lake

Hulakon River

Burroughs Bay

Grant Creek

Fitzgibbon Cove

Point Whaley

Saks Cove

Disappearing Lake

Swedish Meadows

Mt. Reid

Grace Lake

Manzanita Trail

Manzanita Lake

New Eddystone Rock

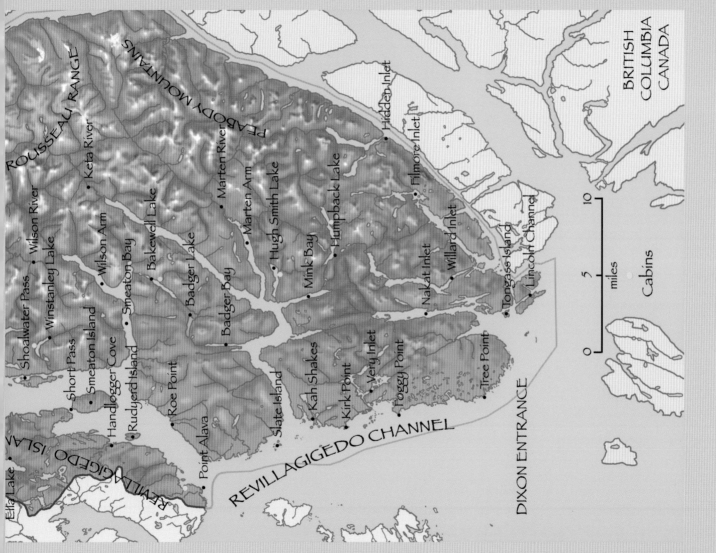

SOUTHEAST ALASKA

BRITISH
COLUMBIA
CANADA

Hidden Inlet

Filmore Inlet

Willard Inlet

Nakat Inlet

Lincoln Channel

Tongass Island

Tree Point

Foggy Point

Very Inlet

Kirk Point

Kah Shakes

Slate Island

Point Alava

Roe Point

Rudyerd Island

Handlogger Cove

Smeaton Island

Short Pass

Shoalwater Pass

Ella Lake

REVILLAGIGEDO ISLAND

REVILLAGIGEDO CHANNEL

DIXON ENTRANCE

Wilson River

Winstanley Lake

Wilson Arm

Smeaton Bay

Bakewell Lake

Badger Lake

Badger Bay

Keta River

Marten River

Marten Arm

Hugh Smith Lake

Mink Bay

Humpback Lake

ROUSSEAU RANGE

PEABODY MOUNTAINS

Cabins

0   5   10
miles

Photographed and written by: Chip Porter
Concept, text, and proof editor: Nick Jans
Photo editor: Chip Porter
Cover design: Elizabeth Watson
Book design: Elizabeth Watson and Chip Porter
Map: Terry Pyles
Printing Managed by: Star Print Brokers, Inc., Bellevue, Washington
Publisher: Chip Porter

Single copies of Misty Fjords National Monument Wilderness can be purchased
for $24.95 plus $5.05 for shipping and handling. Retail discounts are available
for stores.

Chip Porter can be reached at P.O. Box 7844, Ketchikan, Alaska 99901.
Phone: (907) 225-2447
E-mail: chip@kpunet.net
Website: www.chipporteralaska.com

ISBN 10: 1-57833-371-7   ISBN 13: 978-1-57833-371-4

Printed in South Korea
First Printing: April 2007
Second Printing: December 2007
Third Printing: April 2012